IELTS WRITING TASK-1 SAMPLES FOR BEGINNERS

GET 7.5+ BANDS WITH IN 30 DAYS PRACTICE

AF565309

RANJOT SINGH CHAHAL

Copyright © Ranjot Singh Chahal
All Rights Reserved.

ISBN 979-888530748-2

This book has been published with all efforts taken to make the material error-free after the consent of the author. However, the author and the publisher do not assume and hereby disclaim any liability to any party for any loss, damage, or disruption caused by errors or omissions, whether such errors or omissions result from negligence, accident, or any other cause.

While every effort has been made to avoid any mistake or omission, this publication is being sold on the condition and understanding that neither the author nor the publishers or printers would be liable in any manner to any person by reason of any mistake or omission in this publication or for any action taken or omitted to be taken or advice rendered or accepted on the basis of this work. For any defect in printing or binding the publishers will be liable only to replace the defective copy by another copy of this work then available.

Contents

1. Writing Task-1 Sample 1
2. Writing Task-1 Sample 3
3. Writing Task-1 Sample 5
4. Writing Task-1 Sample 7
5. Writing Task-1 Sample 9
6. Writing Task-1 Sample 11
7. Writing Task-1 Sample 13
8. Writing Task-1 Sample 15
9. Writing Task-1 Sample 17
10. Writing Task-1 Sample 19
11. Writing Task-1 Sample 21
12. Writing Task-1 Sample 23
13. Writing Task-1 Sample 25
14. Writing Task-1 Sample 27
15. Writing Task-1 Sample 29
16. Writing Task-1 Sample 31
17. Writing Task-1 Sample 33
18. Writing Task-1 Sample 35
19. Writing Task-1 Sample 37
20. Writing Task-1 Sample 39
21. Writing Task-1 Sample 41
22. Writing Task-1 Sample 43
23. Writing Task-1 Sample 45
24. Writing Task-1 Sample 47
25. Writing Task-1 Sample 49
26. Writing Task-1 Sample 51
27. Writing Task-1 Sample 53
28. Writing Task-1 Sample 55

Contents

29. Writing Task-1 Sample 58

30. Writing Task-1 Sample 60

CHAPTER I

Writing Task-1 Sample

The graph gives information about the age of the population of Iceland between 1990 and 2020.

Summarise the information by selecting and reporting the main features, and make comparisons where relevant.

Write at least 150 words.

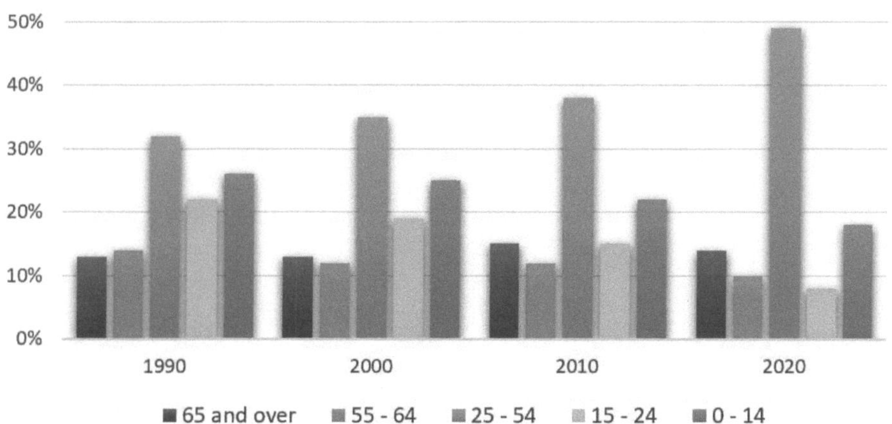

Model answer

The bar chart compares the different ages of people living in Iceland between 1990 and 2020.

All in all, the size of the 25-54 age group increased the most over the period while the size of the two younger age groups decreased a little bit. The number of people in the two older age groups stayed about the same.

The 25-54 age group grew from approximately a third of the population in 1990 to nearly half of the population in 2020.

The older two age groups did not increase or decrease much. The size of the 65 and over age group remained at about 13%, whereas the size of the 55 -64 age group only fell from about 14% to about 10% of the population.

By contrast, the 0-14 age group fell from just over 25% in 1990 to just under 20% in 2020. Similarly, the 15-24 age group dropped from just over 20% of the population in 1990 to just under 10% of the population in 2020.

(168 words)

CHAPTER II

Writing Task-1 Sample

The tables below show people's reasons for giving up smoking, and when they intend to give up.

Summarise the information by selecting and reporting the main features, and make comparisons where relevant.

Write at least 150 words.

TOP 5 REASONS FOR WANTING TO GIVE UP SMOKING				
Reasons for waiting to give up	Number of cigarettes smoked per day			
	20+	**10 - 19**	**Fewer than 10**	**Total**
	%	%	%	%
Better for health in general	64	73	74	71
Less risk of getting smoking-related illnesses	27	28	21	25
Present health problems	19	10	10	12
Financial considerations	31	36	25	31
Family pressure	14	13	20	16

WHEN SMOKERS INTEND TO GIVE UP SMOKING				
When	Number of cigarettes smoked per day			
	20+	**10 - 19**	**Fewer than 10**	**Total**
	%	%	%	%
Within the next month	8	9	21	12
Within the next 6 months	26	32	46	35
Within the next year	22	23	18	21
Total that intend to give up	60	73	79	71
Do not intend to give up	40	27	21	29

Model answer

The two tables together give a snapshot of the reasons people choose to stop smoking and when they intend to give up.

The main reason smokers give for stopping is for general health (71%), with financial considerations (31%) and the risk of smoking-related diseases (25%) being the next two most popular reasons. One fact to highlight from this table is that almost twice the percentage of heavy smokers cite present health problems as the reason compared to light smokers.

According to the second table, the majority of smokers questioned (71%) intended to give up, with light smokers more inclined to stop (79%) than heavy smokers (60%). 35% of smokers said they were planning to give up within the next six months and only 12% said they were prepared to try within the following month. Although only 29% of smokers on average were unwilling to give up, heavy smokers were almost twice as unwilling to try as light smokers, which perhaps reflects the level of addiction in the former group.

(169 words)

CHAPTER III

Writing Task-1 Sample

The table below shows the changes in some household types in Canada from 1984 to 2020.

Summarise the information by selecting and reporting the main features, and make comparisons where relevant.

Write at least 150 words.

PEOPLE IN HOUSEHOLDS BY TYPE OF HOUSEHOLD AND FAMILY					
Canada: household types	Percentages				
	1984	**1994**	**2004**	**2014**	**2020**
One person	6	8	11	12	12
One-family households					
Couple					
No children	19	20	23	25	25
Dependent children	52	47	41	39	36
Non-dependent children	10	10	11	9	9
Lone parent	4	6	10	12	12

Model answer

The table shows the changes in household types in Canada at 10-year intervals from 1984 to 2014 and again in 2020.

There has been a steady increase in households without children during this period. One-person households doubled from 6% in 1984 to 12% in 2020, whilst the percentage of couples with no children rose from 19% in 1984 to 23% in 2004 and to 25% in 2014. However, this figure levelled out in 2020. Even bigger changes have occurred when it comes to couples with dependent children. This category shrank from 52% in 1984 to 36% in 2020. In contrast, the percentage of lone parents trebled over the same period, rising from 4% in 1984 to 12% in 2020. The percentage of families with non-dependent children has remained more stable: 10% in 1984, rising only 1%

over the next 20 years before falling to 9% in 2014.

In conclusion, the table shows definite patterns of change within the Canadian family over the past 40 years, in particular the decline in the traditional. model of one couple with dependent children.

(179 words)

CHAPTER IV

Writing Task-1 Sample

The charts show projections for global production by sector in 2040 and 2060.

Summarise the information by selecting and reporting the main features, and make comparisons where relevant.

Write at least 150 words.

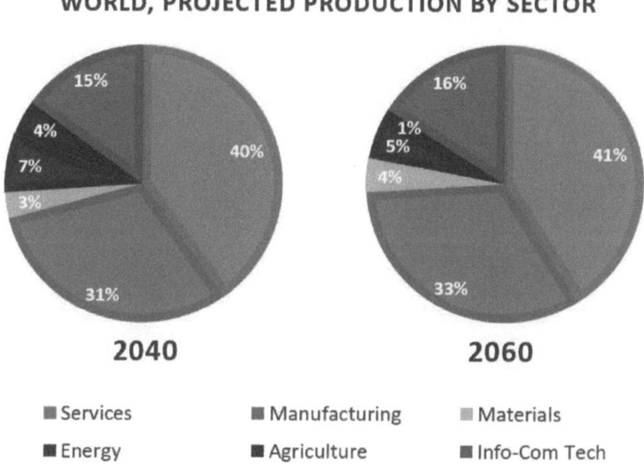

Model answer

The charts show projections for global production by sector in 2040 and 2060. Generally speaking, there is little change in the projected proportion of production by the various sectors in the two years, with manufacturing and services being the most dominant.

It is forecast that the services and manufacturing sectors together will account for more than half of global production in 2040 and 2060, 71% (40% and 31%) and 74% (41% and 33%) respectively. By contrast, the proportion of production from energy is expected to decline from 7% in 2040 to 5% in 2060, a drop of approximately one third. It is also anticipated that there will be a similar dramatic drop for agriculture production from

4% to 1% with production in materials, by contrast, comprising 4% in 2060 compared to 3% in 2040.

As regards info-communications and technology, there is expected to be little difference in the proportion of production the sector constitutes, with a slight rise from 15% to 16% over the period.

(165 words)

CHAPTER V

Writing Task-1 Sample

The table below shows the estimated literacy rates by region and gender for 2000-2004.

Summarise the information by selecting and reporting the main features, and make comparisons where relevant.

Write at least 150 words.

	Total	Male	Female
World	82.2%	87.2%	77.3%
Africa	62.5%	71.6%	53.9%
Americas	93.6%	94.1%	93.2%
Asia	79.3%	85.9%	72.5%
Europe	98.8%	99.2%	98.5%
Ocenia	93.4%	94.2%	92.7%

Model answer

The table shows estimated literacy rates for men and women in 2000-2004 in five regions: Africa, the Americas, Asia, Europe and Oceania. It also shows average world literacy rates for both genders for the same years.

According to the table, Europe has the highest literacy rates, reaching almost 99%. There is virtually no difference in literacy rates for European men and women.

In Oceania and the Americas, the figures for both men and women are almost the same. In both regions over 93% of the population is literate.

In both Asia and Africa, there are considerable differences in literacy rates between men and women. In Asia, only 72.5% of women are literate, whereas the figure for Asian men is 13% higher. In Africa, the gap is nearly double, with 53.9% of all African women being literate and 71.6% of the African men being able to read and write.

Overall, around 82% of the world population is literate. In Europe, Oceania and the Americas the literacy rates are the highest, with over 90% of the population able to read and write. Asia and Africa have lower literacy rates than the other regions in the graph.

(194 words)

CHAPTER VI

Writing Task-1 Sample

The chart gives information on the percentage of women going into higher education in five countries for the years 1980 and 2015.

Summarise the information by selecting and reporting the main features, and make comparisons where relevant.

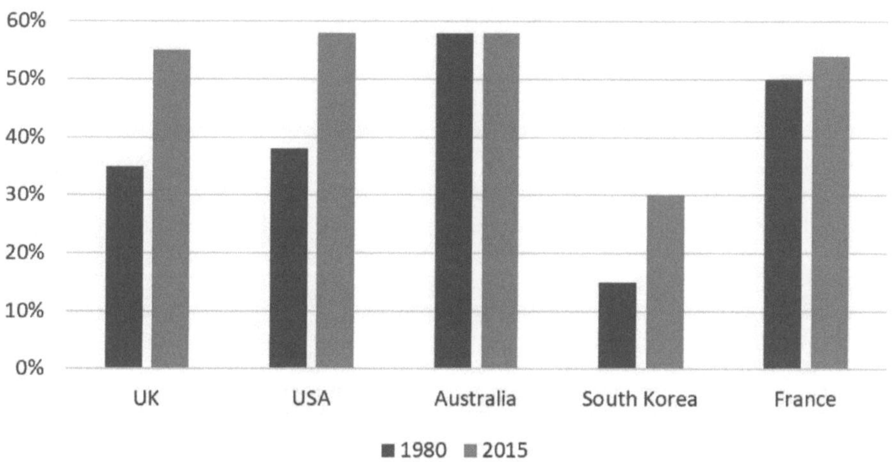

Write at least 150 words.

Model answer

The bar chart shows the percentage of females entering higher education in the years 1980 and 2015. The chart shows the percentages in five countries, the UK, the USA, Australia, South Korea and France. Overall, the proportion of women in higher education increased in the five countries.

In general, there were more female students in 2015 than in 1980, with more than half of women in higher education in all of the countries apart from South Korea. In four of the countries, the percentage of women going into higher education rose.

The most dramatic change was in South Korea, where the percentage doubled from 15% to 30%. The smallest change was seen in France, where the number increased only from 50% to 54%. The only country in which there was not an increase was Australia. Although the percentage of Australian women going into higher education remained the same at 58%, this was the highest in 1980 and equal highest with the USA in 2015.

(164 words)

CHAPTER VII

Writing Task-1 Sample

The chart and graph below give information about participants who have entered the Olympics since it began.

Summarise the information by selecting and reporting the main features, and make comparisons where relevant.

Write at least 150 words.

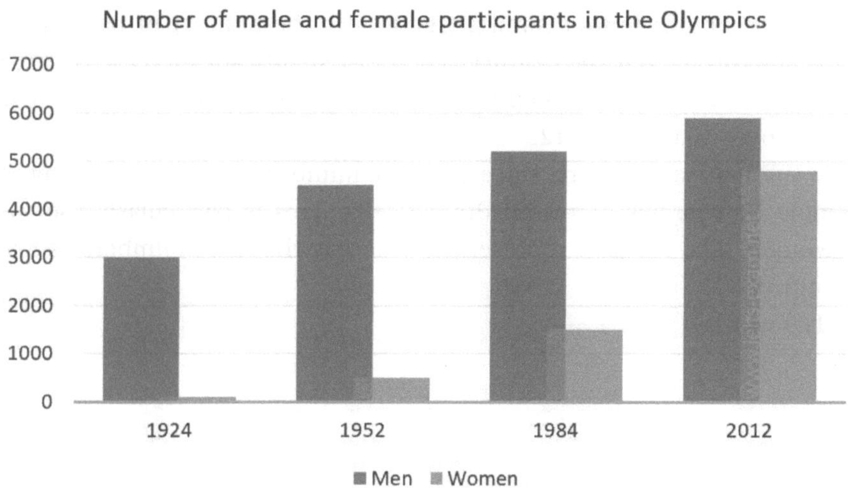

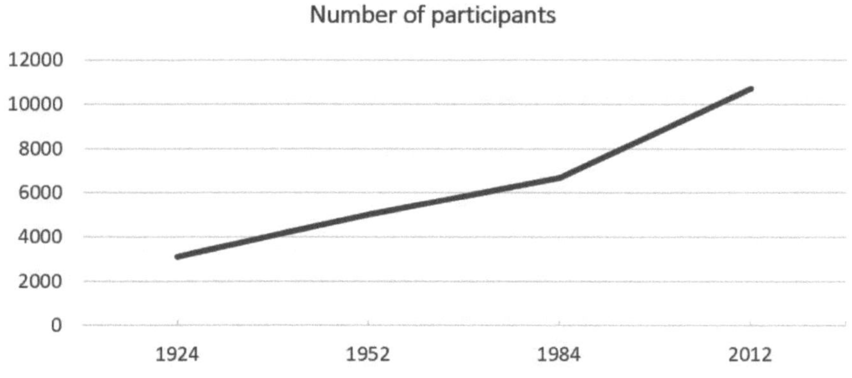

Model answer

The two charts give information about the gender and number of athletes who have entered the Games since they started. The bar chart illustrates the number of men and women entering the Games, whereas the line graph shows the number of participants.

It is evident from the bar chart that, until 2012, there were always significantly more men entering the Games than women. In 1924 and 1952, there were hardly any women entering the Games, yet in 1952 there were over 4,000 male participants. In 2012, however, the number of female athletes rose significantly to nearly 5,000, only approximately 1,000 lower than male participants.

The line graph shows a similar trend, with the number of participants increasing throughout the century. The most significant increase occurred between 1984 and 2012, when the number of athletes rose from just over 6,000 to over 10,000 in 2012.

To summarise therefore, since 1924 the number of athletes entering the Olympic Games, has increased dramatically. This is particularly the case for women, who are now represented in nearly the same numbers as male participants.

(179 words)

CHAPTER VIII

Writing Task-1 Sample

The bar charts below give information on road transport in a number of European countries.

Summarise the information by selecting and reporting the main features, and make comparisons where relevant.

Write at least 150 words.

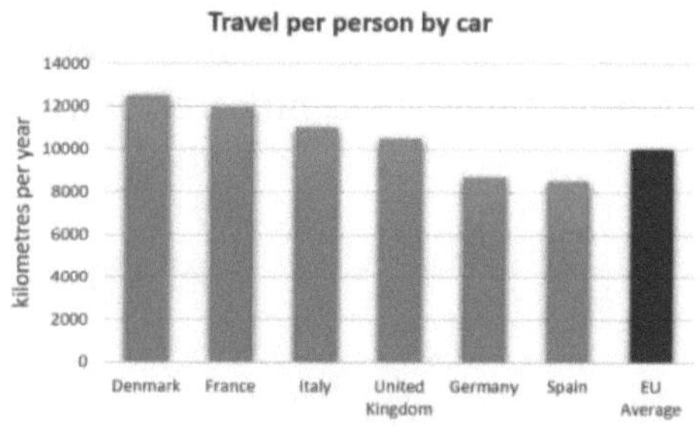

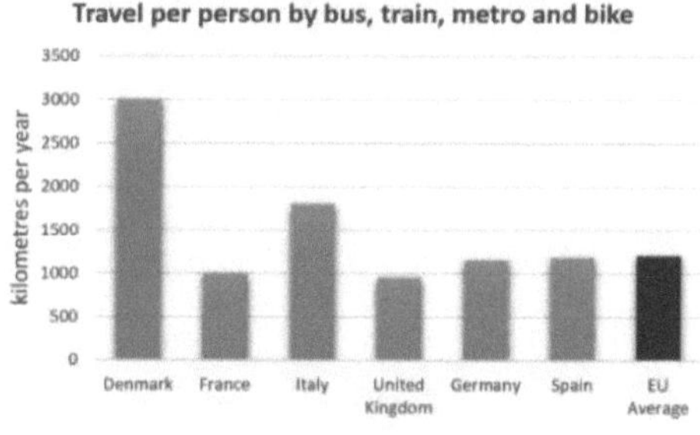

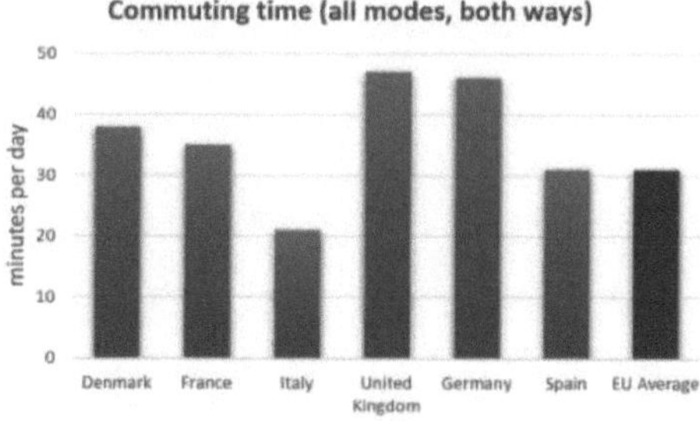

Model answer

The bar charts give information about methods of travel and commuting times for six European countries, as well as the average figure for the European Union. From the information, we can see that car use is highest in Denmark at about 12,500 kilometres per person a year, and lowest in Spain and Germany.

Perhaps surprisingly, the Danish also make far greater use of alternative transport than people in other countries, travelling over 3,000 kilometres a year by bus, tram, metro or bike, which is more than double the EU average. By comparison, the British and French travel less than a third of that distance by public transport.

When it comes to commuting times, British drivers spend about 47 minutes each day travelling to work, which is more than any other country. In Denmark and Italy, on the other hand, where many more people use public transport, commuting times are significantly lower.

(151 words)

CHAPTER IX

Writing Task-1 Sample

The graph gives information about male and female gym membership between 1980 and 2010.

Summarise the information by selecting and reporting the main features, and make comparisons where relevant.

Write at least 150 words.

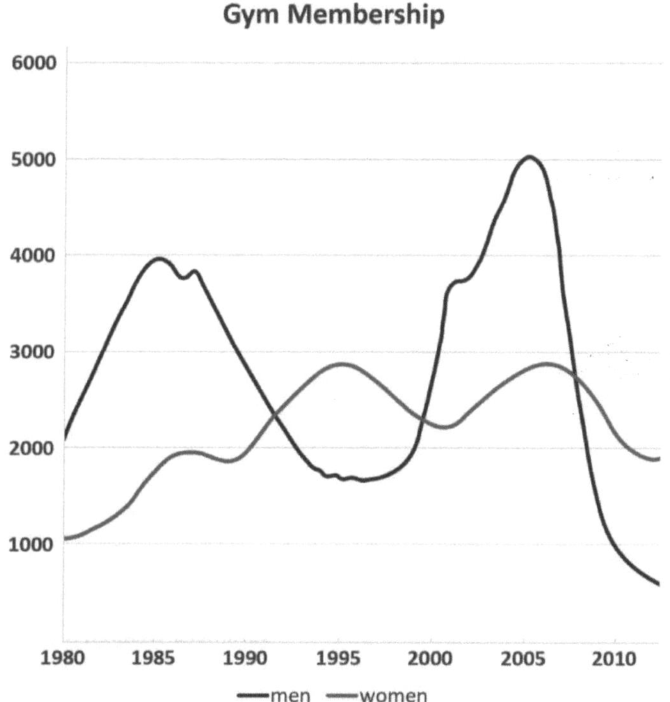

Model answer

The line graph shows male and female gym membership over a thirty-year period. The vertical axis represents the number of members in units of 1,000. The horizontal axis represents the period from 1980 to 2010.

Overall, the graph indicates that there were greater fluctuations in gym membership among men than among women. The number of male members started the period at just over two thousand and reached highs of four thousand in 1985 and five thousand around 2005. The lowest rates were between 1993 and 1997 and more recently in 2010 when the rate dipped as low as one thousand.

Female gym membership began lower at one thousand, doubled by 1984, and then fluctuated between two and three thousand for the remainder of the period. When male rates were at their lowest, female rates were higher. This was particularly true between 1993 and 1997 when over three thousand women held gym membership.

In brief, there were marked differences in rates of male and female gym memberships in the period covered.

(170 words)

CHAPTER X

Writing Task-1 Sample

The pie charts compare ways of accessing the news in Canada and Australia.

Summarise the information by selecting and reporting the main features, and make comparisons where relevant.

Write at least 150 words.

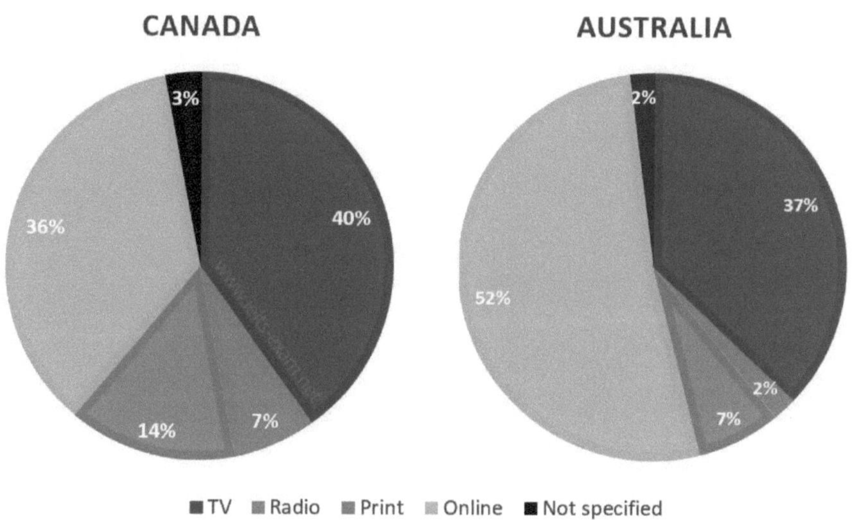

Model answer

The pie charts show the principle ways of finding out the news in two different countries, Canada and Australia. The two nations show broadly similar patterns, though there are some differences, both significant and minor.

One of the most prominent features of this data is that, while in Canada over a third of people access the news online, in Australia the figure is more than half, at 52%. It is apparent that viewing the TV news is popular in both countries, with about two fifths of Canadian population favouring this mode of delivery and only 3% fewer in Australia. One major difference between Canada and Australia is that over twice as many people read the news in print in the former, compared with the latter. The figures are 14% and 7%

respectively. Similarly, listening to the news on the radio is preferred by three times more people in Canada than in Australia.

Overall, it can be said that the high levels of internet use in Australia mean that other methods such as radio and print are used less in comparison with Canada.

(182 words)

CHAPTER XI

Writing Task-1 Sample

The graph below shows the percentage of part-time workers in each country of the United Kingdom in 1980 and 2010.

Summarise the information by selecting and reporting the main features, and make comparisons where relevant.

Write at least 150 words.

Model answer

The bar chart shows the percentage of people who have part-time jobs in the countries that make up the United Kingdom, both in 1980 and in 2010. There'has generally been a small increase in part-time workers from 1980 to 2010, except in Northern Ireland. The graph also shows that England and Wales have far more part-time workers than Northern Ireland and Scotland.

In 1980, 25% of people in England worked part time. The only country with a greater percentage of part-time workers was Wales, with around 33% working part time. Both countries saw an increase in the percentage of people working part time in 2010. In England, the percentage rose to over 30% and in Wales percentage rose to just over 35%.

Scotland had the smallest percentage of part-time workers in 1980, with just over ten per cent. However, this rose to almost 20% in 2010 which is a large increase. Lastly, Northern Ireland was the only country which had a decreasing percentage of part-time workers. In 1980, it had around 15% of people in part-time work. This decreased by a couple of per cent in 2010.

(187 words)

CHAPTER XII

Writing Task-1 Sample

The chart below shows the proportions of graduates from Brighton University in 2019 entering different employment sectors.

Summarise the information by selecting and reporting the main features, and make comparisons where relevant.

Write at least 150 words.

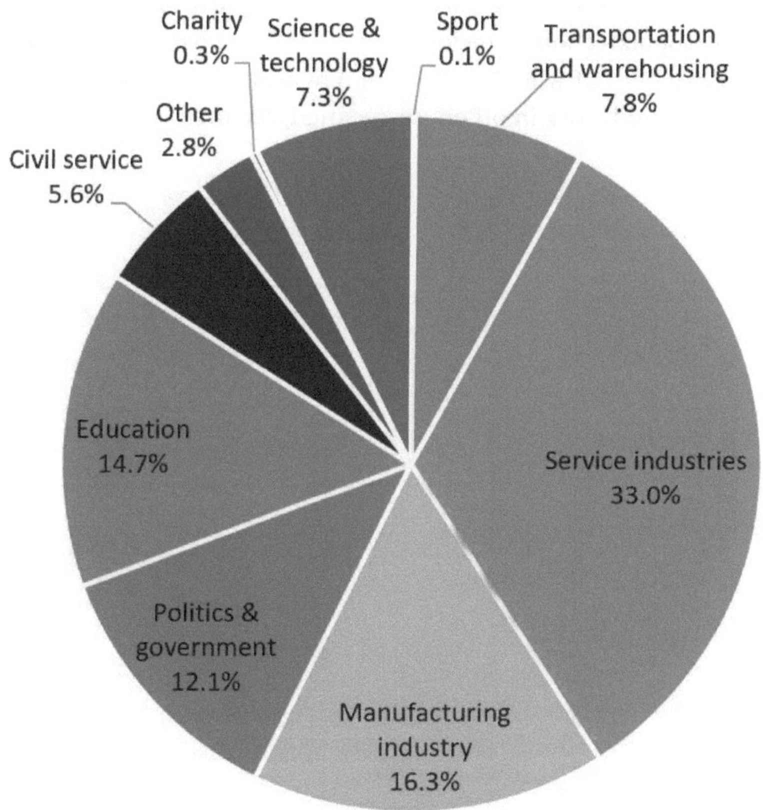

Enter Caption

Model answer

The pie chart illustrates the career choices of Brighton University's 2019 graduates, giving the percentages who worked in each of various sectors after finishing university. Overwhelmingly, industry and government were the most popular choices.

Just under half the students went into industry, with service industries attracting more Brighton graduates than any other sector by far — almost a third (33.0%). About half that number (16.3%) took jobs in manufacturing.

Politics and public service were the next most popular choice, accounting for nearly a fifth of graduates. Just over 12% went into politics and a further 5.6% chose the civil service. The other significant career choices were education (about 15%) and two others: transportation and warehousing, with 7.8%; and science and technology with 7.3%.

The least popular choices included work in the charitable sector and careers in sport, both of which were chosen by well under 1% of graduates. Finally, 2.8% entered work in other, unspecified, sectors.

(155 words)

CHAPTER XIII

Writing Task-1 Sample

The diagram illustrates how bees produce honey.

Summarise the information by selecting and reporting the main features, and make comparisons where relevant.

Write at least 150 words.

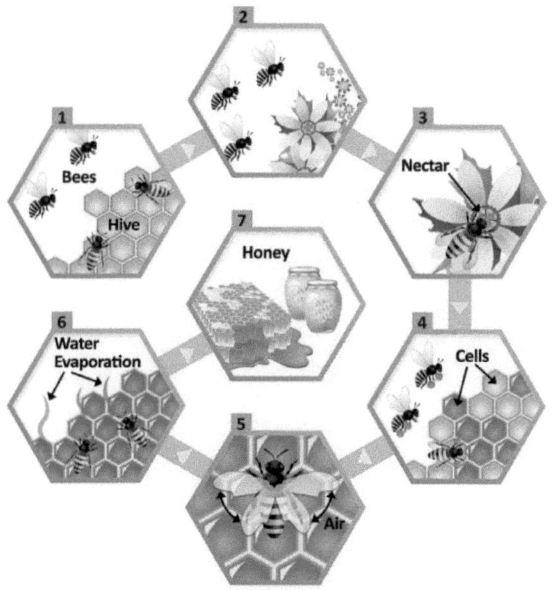

Nectar: a sweet liquid produced by flowers

Hive: a container where bees live

Evaporation: water changing to gas

Model answer

The diagram shows the seven most important stages in the making of honey by bees. The process begins with the honey bees building a hive, and then finishes when the honey is ready to be collected and used.

Firstly, the bees have to build a container. This is called a hive and it consists of many individually built cells. Next, the bees leave the hive in order to search for flowers. When they find a suitable flower, they collect the nectar from it, which is used to make honey.

The nectar is then taken back to the hive where the production process can begin. First, it is put into cells. Then, following this, the nectar must be cooled down. In order to do this, the bees fan the nectar-filled cells with their wings. As a result, the nectar loses its water content and then finally, the honey is produced.

(150 words)

CHAPTER XIV

Writing Task-1 Sample

The maps show improvements that have been made to a university campus between 2010 and the present day.

Summarise the information by selecting and reporting the main features, and make comparisons where relevant.

Write at least 150 words.

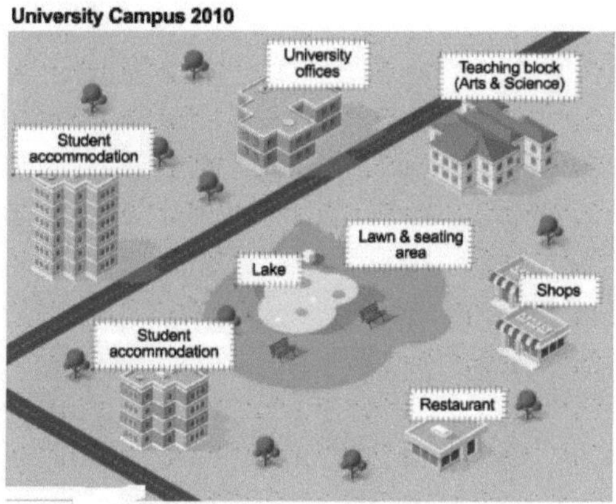

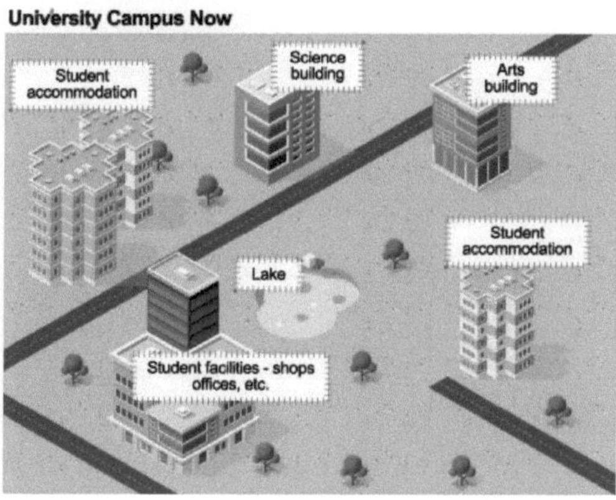

Model answer

The two maps show the development of a university campus from 2010 to the present day. It can be seen from the maps that the campus has been improved and extended, with much more student accommodation and facilities than previously.

Firstly, the number of student accommodation buildings has been increased in number and size. A previous accommodation block south of the lake has been destroyed and replaced by a new building for students, which includes shops and offices. In addition, the teaching facilities have been extended. The previous single teaching block has been changed into a block only for arts subjects and there is a new building for the sciences to the north of the campus. This has replaced the old university offices. The lawn and outside seating area which were next to the lake have been removed. The lake, however, has remained and is still the central point of the campus.

(152 words)

CHAPTER XV

Writing Task-1 Sample

The graph shows the number of visitors to four international museums between 1980 and 2015.

Summarise the information by selecting and reporting the main features, and make comparisons where relevant.

Write at least 150 words.

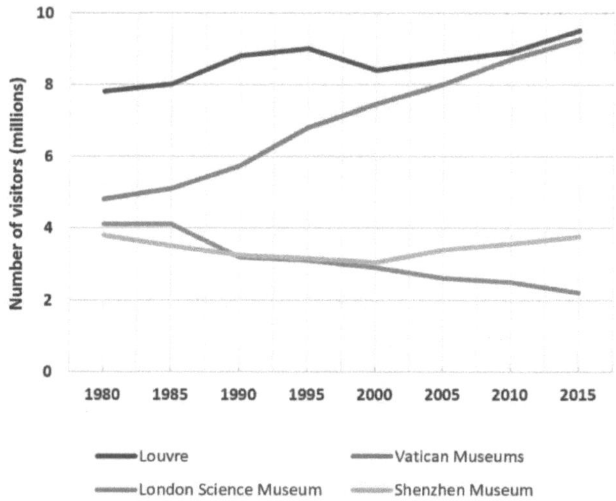

Model answer

The line graph shows how many people visited four museums in different countries in the world between 1980 and 2015.

All in all, the Louvre Museum was the most popular, with between approximately 8 and 9 million visitors each year. The least popular were the Shenzhen and the London Science Museum, with no more than 4 million visitors each year.

The number of visitors to the London Science Museum decreased slowly from just over 4 million in 1980 to around 2 million in 2015. By contrast, the visitors to the Vatican Museum increased from just under 5 million in

1980 to around 9 million in 2015.

In addition, the number of visitors to the Shenzhen Museum stayed about the same over the thirty-five-year period. They fell from just under 4 million in 1980 to just over 3 million in 2000 and then rose to just under 4 million again in 2015.

(151 words)

CHAPTER XVI

Writing Task-1 Sample

The bar charts below show the percentages of men and women in employment in three countries in 2005 and 2015.

Summarise the information by selecting and reporting the main features, and make comparisons where relevant.

Write at least 150 words.

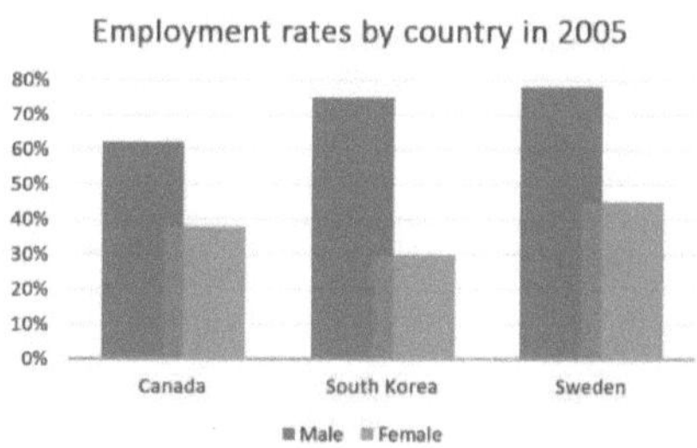

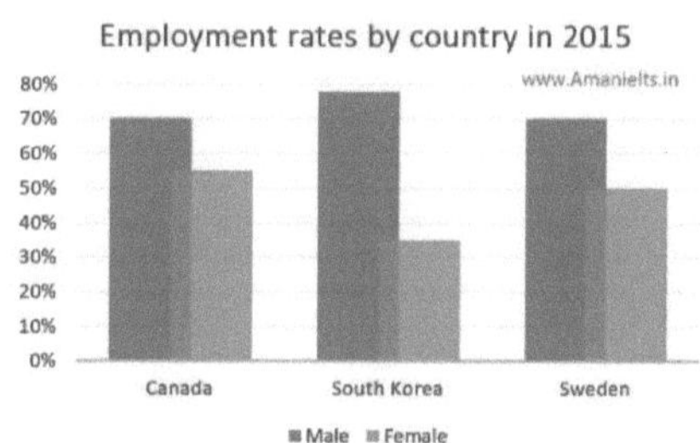

Model answer

The two charts show the percentages of men and women in employment in three countries in the years 2005 and 2015. In general, we can see that the percentages of working people increased, with the proportion of women showing the most significant rise.

In all of the countries covered, and in both years, the number of men in employment was greater than the number of women. South Korea has the highest rate of male employment – approximately 75% in 2005, rising slightly to about 78% in 2015 – and Canada has the lowest – just over 60% in 2005 and 70% in 2015.

The proportion of women in employment was lower than men in all of the countries covered over the two years. It was below 50% everywhere in 2005, but the figures had risen by 2015. In Canada, over half of the women were working, and in Sweden the figure was exactly 50%. In contrast, the number of South Korean women who were working was only about 35% compared with a percentage which was more than double for men at over 70%.

(180 words)

CHAPTER XVII

Writing Task-1 Sample

The pie charts below show the devices people in the 18 to 25 age group use to watch television in Canada in two different years.

Summarise the information by selecting and reporting the main features, and make comparisons where relevant.

Write at least 150 words.

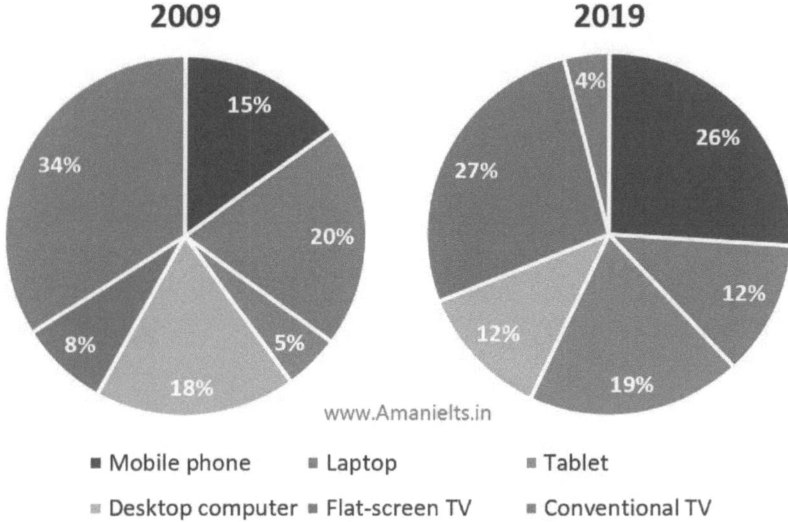

Model answer

The two charts illustrate the appliances that young adults in Canada use to watch television programmes and how this has changed over the ten-year period from 2009 to 2019. One of the key changes over this decade is the transition from conventional televisions to flat-screens, with the former falling from 34% to 4% and the latter rising from 8% to 27% for the period, making it the number one television device. The latter has replaced the former as the most popular TV viewing device.

Another general trend is that younger people are now watching television on smaller, more portable devices than in 2009. In particular, the use of mobile phones and tablets for viewing purposes has increased by almost three quarters to 26% and tablet use seeing an almost four-fold increase to 19%. This trend is reinforced by the number of 18 to 25-year-olds using computers for the TV viewing. Both desktop and laptop computers saw substantial falls in usage (around a third for both).

Overall then, it can be said that the two pie charts suggest the TV viewing habits in Canada over the period saw a move away from older devices and towards more modern equivalents.

(198 words)

CHAPTER XVIII

Writing Task-1 Sample

The table below shows the percentage participation of women in senior management in three companies between 1975 and 2015.

Summarise the information by selecting and reporting the main features, and make comparisons where relevant.

Write at least 150 words.

Percentage participation of women in senior management positions

www.Amanielts.in

	Eldan Ltd	Bamforth Ltd	Finsbury Ltd
1975	3%	9%	16%
1980	3%	11%	14%
1985	14%	13%	15%
1990	28%	15%	22%
2000	33%	17%	20%
2015	64%	46%	26%

Model answer

The table shows the percentage of women in senior management positions in three companies from 1975 to 2015.

While more women were in senior positions at Finsbury Ltd than the other two companies in 1975 at 16%, the trend was fairly erratic with a 2% drop to 14% in 1980, followed by a rise of 1% five years later. In 1990, women held 7% more top management jobs than in 1985. After a slight drop back to 20% in 2000, by 2015 26% of top posts were filled by women.

By contrast, at Eldan Ltd women fared much better. In 1975, 3% of senior posts were occupied by women with no change five years on. By 1985, the figure had increased to 14%, doubling to 28% in 1990. Ten years afterwards, there was a 5% increase in female senior management jobs with a near twofold jump in 2015 to stand at 64%, the highest for the three companies.

The situation was less remarkable at Bamforth Ltd than the other two firms except for the year 2015. In 1975, the percentage of senior posts held by women was 9% climbing at the rate of 2% in each subsequent period until 2000, after which it leapt to 46%.

From the data, it is clear that women dominated senior posts at Eldan by 2015.

(221 words)

CHAPTER XIX

Writing Task-1 Sample

The graphs below show the number of medals won by the top five countries in the summer and winter Olympics.

Summarise the information by selecting and reporting the main features, and make comparisons where relevant.

Write at least 150 words.

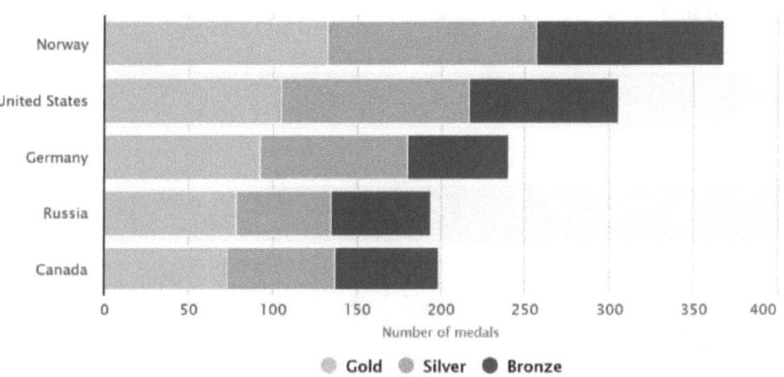

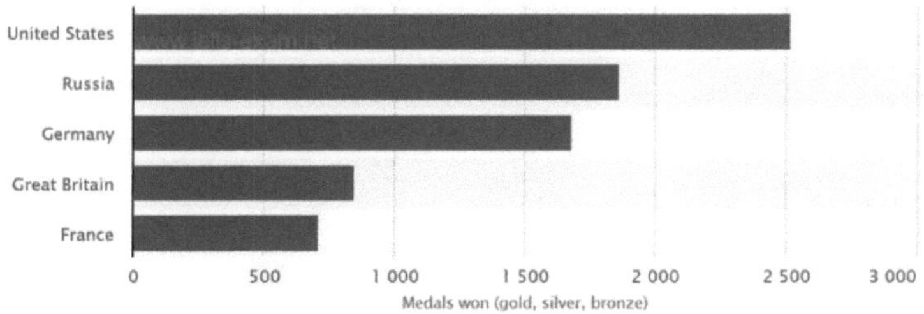

Model answer

The first bar chart shows which countries have won the most medals in the winter Olympics. It also states how many gold, silver and bronze medals each country has achieved. In contrast, the second graph shows which nations have won the most medals in the summer Olympics.

Overall, the first graph shows that in the winter Olympics, Norway has gained the most medals, winning approximately an equal number of gold, silver and bronze medals. It has won about 370 medals, whereas Canada, in fifth place, has won approximately 200 medals.

The results of the summer Olympics are quite different, however, with the USA having won the most medals. Overall, the USA has won just over 2,500 medals, a much higher number than the other four countries on the graph. Russia is the second highest, winning approximately 1,800 medals.

To summarise, the bar charts illustrate how many medals the highest-ranking countries have won in the summer and winter Olympics. The results of each Olympics are very different, with the USA, Russia and Germany being successful in both.

(176 words)

CHAPTER XX

Writing Task-1 Sample

The chart below gives information about global population percentages and distribution of wealth by region.

Summarise the information by selecting and reporting the main features, and make comparisons where relevant.

Write at least 150 words.

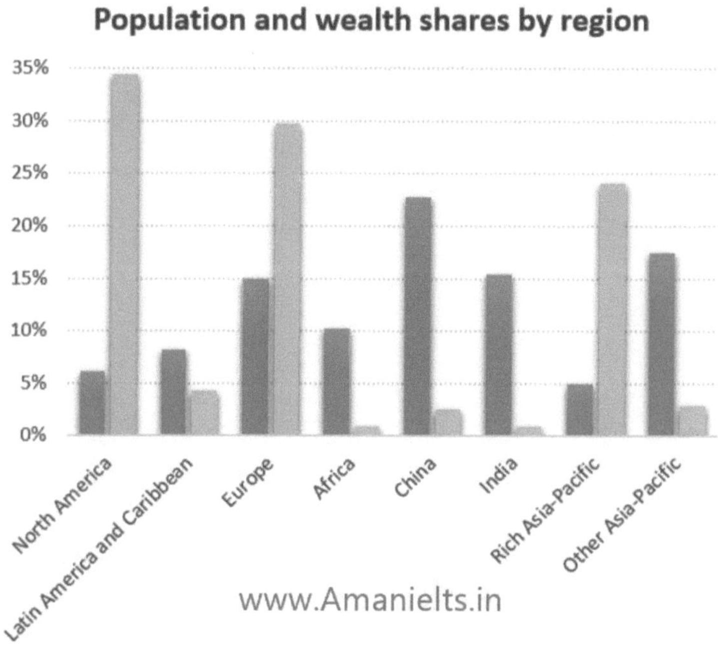

Model answer

The chart compares population shares in various regions of the world with the distribution of wealth in these same regions. It can be seen that wealth is heavily concentrated in North America, Europe, and high income Asia-Pacific countries which together account for almost 90% of global wealth.

Even though North America has only approximately 6% of the world's population, it boasts nearly 34% of global wealth. A similar situation can be seen in Europe, which has 15% of the global population but 30% of global wealth, and high income Asia-Pacific countries with 5% of the world's population but 24% of its wealth.

In contrast, the overall share of wealth owned by people in Africa, China, India, and other lower income countries in Asia is considerably less than their population share, sometimes by a factor of more than ten. This is most striking in India, where 16% of the world's population own only 1% of the world's wealth and in China, which has the highest percentage of global population (24%) but only 3% of the world's wealth.

(176 words)

CHAPTER XXI

Writing Task-1 Sample

The graph shows data on the manufacture of passenger cars in 2015.

Summarise the information by selecting and reporting the main features, and make comparisons where relevant.

Write at least 150 words.

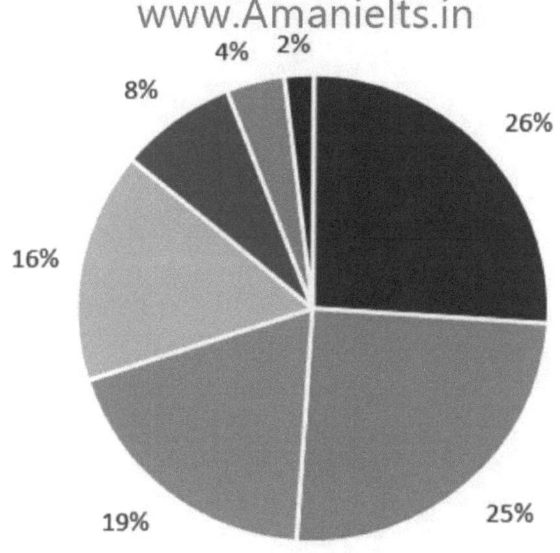

Model answer

The pie chart gives the percentage of passenger cars manufactured by different regions of the world. For the purposes of this data set, the world is divided into seven regions.

What stands out is that the regions of Greater China and Europe lead the way in terms of the manufacture of passenger cars, with 26% and 25% respectively. By contrast, very few cars are produced in the Middle East and Africa: just 2% originate from that area.

Turning next to the Americas, a sharp contrast can be seen between the Northern and Southern parts of the continent. Whereas North America can boast 19% of the world's passenger car production, South America manufactures just 4% of this type of vehicle.

Finally, moving on to Japan and Korea, despite the fact that they are just two countries rather than a whole region, they account for a sizeable proportion of the total, at 16%.

(151 words)

CHAPTER XXII

Writing Task-1 Sample

The chart below gives information on the percentage of Canadians gave money to charitable organisations by age range for the years 2000 and 2015.

Summarise the information by selecting and reporting the main features, and make comparisons where relevant.

Write at least 150 words.

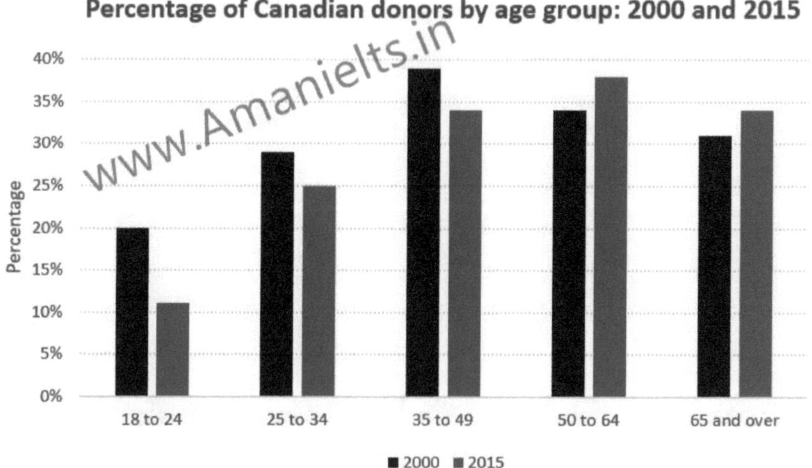

Model answer

The chart examines the levels of donation among people of different ages in Canada.

Overall, a greater proportion of Canadians gave money to charitable organisations in 2000 than in 2015. However, in terms of trends over time, the donor rate did not change in the same way among all age groups.

In 2000, the proportion of Canadians made charitable donations ranged from a high of 39% in the 35-to-49 age group to a low of 20% in the 18-to-24 age group. By 2015, these figures had fallen significantly to 34% and 11% respectively. The rate of donors among the population aged 25 to 34 also decreased from 29% in 2000 to 25% in 2015.

While the proportion of donors aged 18 to 49 declined between 2000 and 2015, the trend followed an opposite direction for older Canadians. For example, among people aged 50 to 64, the share of donors rose by 4% to nearly 38%, which was the highest percentage for 2015. The figure for older seniors aged 65 and over was lower than this, at 34%, but it was still a little higher than the 2000 figure of 31%.

(190 words)

CHAPTER XXIII

Writing Task-1 Sample

The chart below shows the movement of people from rural to urban areas in three countries and predictions for future years.

Summarise the information by selecting and reporting the main features, and make comparisons where relevant.

Write at least 150 words.

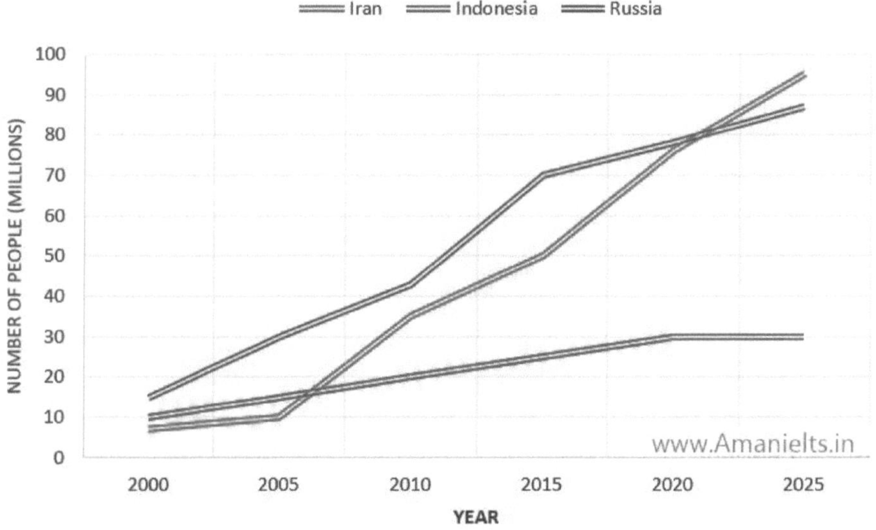

Model answer

The line graph shows the figures in millions for the migration of people from the countryside to cities in three different countries over the period 2000 to 2025, including future predictions. Overall, it is clear that the shift from rural communities towards urban metropolitan areas is upwards.

All three countries began the period with similar numbers of urban migrants. Russia started with the most migrants (around 15 million) and over the period sees significant increases, particularly between 2010 and 2015 (around 42 to 70 million) with this upward trend predicted to continue (reaching approximately 86 million by 2025). Similarly, Iran after a slow start between 2000 and 2005 sees a dramatic rise in urban migration, and after 2015 is predicted to see an even more dramatic increase, surpassing Russia's figures in 2020 reaching around 95 million by 2025. However, Indonesia bucks the trend somewhat. Whilst consistently steady between 2000 and 2020, its growth is far less dramatic than the other two countries (10 to 30 million). Furthermore, post 2020, it is predicted to level off at around 30 million.

To sum up, while all three countries have seen growth up to 2015, only the figures for countries Russia and Iran are predicted to see continued growth up to 2025.

(209 words)

CHAPTER XXIV

Writing Task-1 Sample

The bar chart below shows employment figures in different tourism-related industries between 2009 and 2019.

Summarise the information by selecting and reporting the main features, and make comparisons where relevant.

Write at least 150 words.

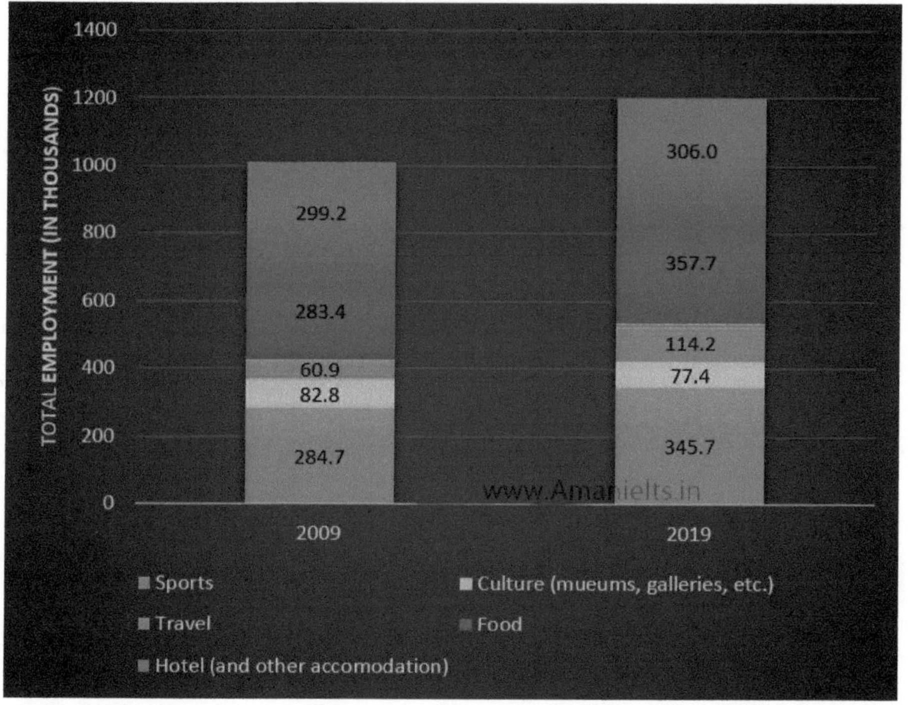

Model answer

The chart provides a breakdown of employment in a number of tourism-related industries over a ten-year period. Overall, we can see that the total level of employment increased by about twenty per cent during the period. However, there was some variation in the figures for the individual sectors. For example, while the travel industry increased its workforce substantially over the decade, there was relatively little growth in that associated with hotels and other tourist accommodation.

Travel represented the biggest area of expansion, having almost doubled its number of employees by 2019. The food industry also saw a significant increase, from 283,000 employees in 2009 to 357,000 in 2019, while the sports industry enjoyed an almost equal level of growth. The least successful sector was culture, including museums and art galleries, where the figures actually fell slightly over the period.

The data suggests that, despite minor fluctuations in the various sectors, employment in the tourism industry as a whole will continue to grow.

(162 words)

CHAPTER XXV

Writing Task-1 Sample

The line graph gives information about the number of Iranian, Greek and Turkish students who enrolled at Sheffield University between 2005 and 2009.

Summarise the information by selecting and reporting the main features, and make comparisons where relevant.

Write at least 150 words.

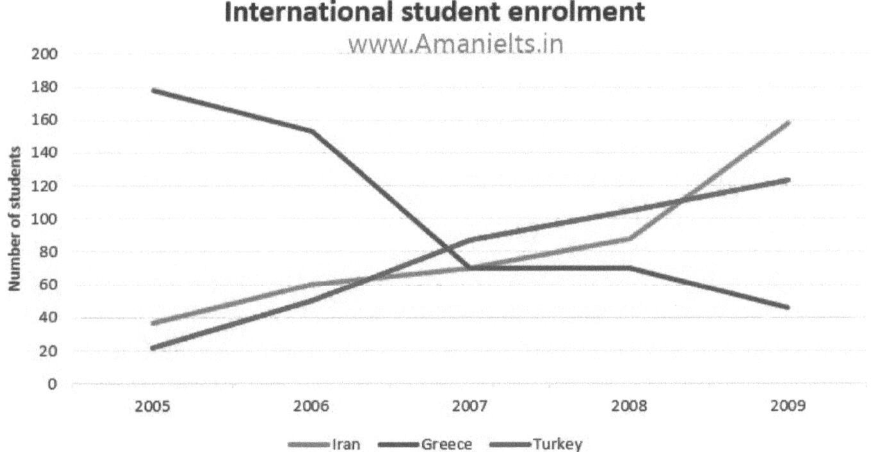

Model answer

The diagram shows the enrolment of Iranian, Greek and Turkish students at Sheffield University from 2005 to 2009. During this period, enrolment of both Iranian and Turkish students rocketed sharply. However, Greek admissions dropped significantly with numbers being almost the reverse of those for Iranian students.

Iranian numbers grew steadily up to 2008 followed by a sharp rise reaching almost 160 students in 2009. Similarly, numbers of Turkish students showed steady growth throughout the period from about 20 in 2005 to over 120 in 2009. In contrast, enrolments of Greek students decreased dramatically from a high of 180 students in 2005 to just about 70 in 2007. Numbers then levelled off throughout 2007 finally dropping again to a low of around 45 in 2009. A further point of interest is that from 2007 to 2008, enrolments from all three countries were very similar, the average difference being approximately 20 students.

Overall, the graph highlights a considerable difference between growth in Iranian and Turkish enrolments but reduction in Greek enrolments.

(169 words)

CHAPTER XXVI

Writing Task-1 Sample

The chart below shows the changes that took place in three different areas of crime in Panama City from 2010 to 2019.

Summarise the information by selecting and reporting the main features, and make comparisons where relevant.

Write at least 150 words.

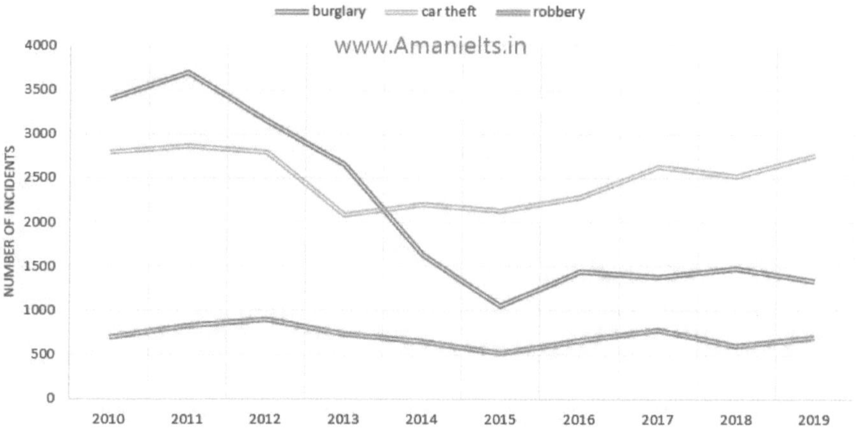

Model answer

This graph illustrates how crime rates altered in Panama City during the period 2010-2019. We can see immediately that the greatest change occurred in the number of burglaries, while incidents of theft remained low but steady.

In 2010, we can see that burglary was the most common crime, with approximately 3,400 reported cases. The figure rose to around 3,700 in 2011, but then there was a downward trend until 2015. At this point the figure stood at just over 1,000 incidents. This rose slightly in 2016, then continued to fluctuate for the remaining period.

In 2010, the number of cars being stolen stood at around 2,800 and followed a similar trend to burglary until 2013. At this point the number rose, standing at around 2,200 in 2014. There was a marginal decrease in the following year, but from then on, the trend was generally upwards.

Finally, robbery has always been a fairly minor problem for Panama City. The number of offences committed changed little over nine years. It is interesting to note that the figure of approximately 700 in 2010 is the same figure for 2019.

(185 words)

CHAPTER XXVII

Writing Task-1 Sample

The graph below shows the number of hours per day on average that children spent watching television between 1950 and 2010.

Summarise the information by selecting and reporting the main features, and make comparisons where relevant.

Write at least 150 words.

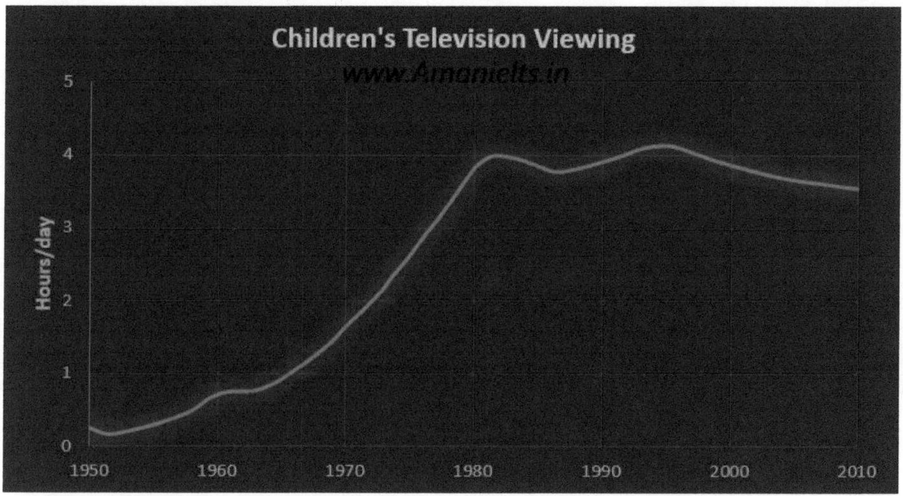

Model answer

The graph shows the number of hours per day on average that children spent watching television. The graph covers the period between 1950 and 2010.

From 1950 to 1960, there was a modest rise in the average number of hours children spent in front of the television set. This was followed by a marked increase from approximately one hour to four hours of viewing per day among children between 1965 and 1982. Over the next five years, there was a decrease. However this trend proved negligible as the viewing figure then rose again marginally, and it reached a peak of over four hours in 1995.

Between 1995 and 2010, there was another modest decline in the hours children spent watching television.

Overall, it can be concluded that there has been a significant rise in television viewing over the sixty-year period, though there is some indication that this trend may be changing.

(151 words)

CHAPTER XXVIII

Writing Task-1 Sample

The graphs below show the post-school qualifications held by Canadians in the age groups 25 to 35 and 45 to 55.

Summarise the information by selecting and reporting the main features, and make comparisons where relevant.

Write at least 150 words.

515,600 Canadians aged between **25** and **35** hold a degree.
Their main fields of study were:

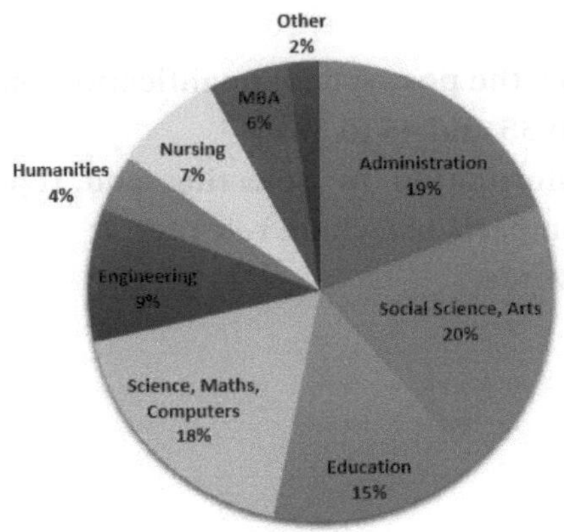

www.Amanielts.in

213,400 Canadians aged between **45** and **55** hold a degree.
Their main fields of study were:

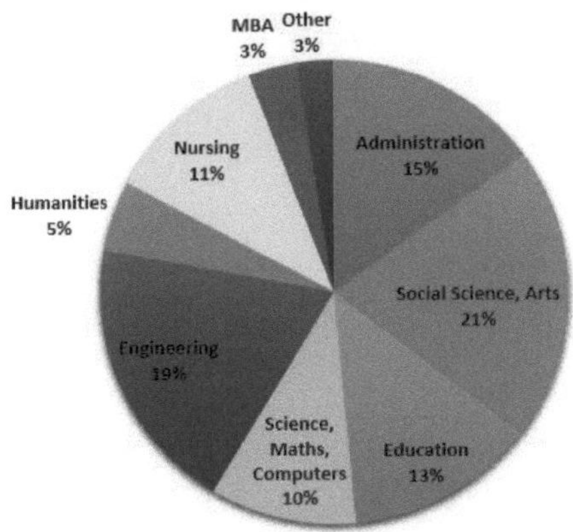

Model answer

These two pie charts show the differences between two groups of Canadians (25 to 35 and 45 to 55 year olds) in terms of their post-school qualifications.

The first point to note is the huge increase in the number of people with qualifications. The younger group is more than two times bigger than the older group (515,600 compared to 213,400).

Comparing the two groups, Humanities and Nursing have experienced an increase in popularity with older graduates; Nursing rose by 4%. However, the biggest gain was made by engineering, which increased from 9% to 19% of the whole.

Some subjects were more popular with the younger age group. The biggest loss in graduate numbers were to Science, Maths and Computers which, as a group, have decreased by 8%. Administration has declined by 4%.

To sum up, the graphs show a more than twofold increase in the number of graduates. The most noticeable change in subject percentages is the increase in the number of engineering graduates.

(164 words)

CHAPTER XXIX

Writing Task-1 Sample

The table below shows top ten countries with largest population in 2019, and how it is projected to change by 2100.

Summarise the information by selecting and reporting the main features, and make comparisons where relevant.

Write at least 150 words.

Top ten countries with largest population, in million

2019		2100 projection	
China	1,439	India	1,551
India	1,380	China	941
USA	331	Nigeria	730
Indonesia	274	USA	478
Pakistan	221	Pakistan	316
Brazil	213	D.R. Congo*	296
Nigeria	206	Indonesia	292
Bangladesh	165	Ethiopia	212
Russia	146	Tanzania	178
Mexico	129	Brazil	177

* Democratic Republic of Congo

www.Amanielts.in

Model answer

The table compares the population of the world's top ten countries in 2019 with projected numbers in 2100.

In 2019, China had the highest population of 1,439 million, with India second on 1,380 million. However, by 2100, India is projected to have the highest population of 1,551 million with China second on 941 million - down 498 million since 2019. Although the USA is projected to increase its population from 331 million to 478 million, it steps down from third to fourth place, being overtaken by Nigeria, which moves up from seventh place with 206 million, to a total of 730 million, representing a massive increase of 524 million. Brazil drops from sixth place in 2019 with 213 million, down to tenth in 2100 on 177 million - a decrease of 36 million.

Three of the ten most populous countries in the world will no longer be among the top ten in 2100, and all three will be supplanted by rapidly growing nations in Africa.

Except for China and Brazil, all other projections show an increase between 2019 and 2100, but there is a significant shuffling of position by some countries, the elimination of others, and the introduction of new contenders for a top-ten placing

(203 words)

CHAPTER XXX

Writing Task-1 Sample

The diagrams below show the main reasons workers chose to work from home and the hours males and females worked at home for the year 2019.

Summarise the information by selecting and reporting the main features, and make comparisons where relevant.

Write at least 150 words.

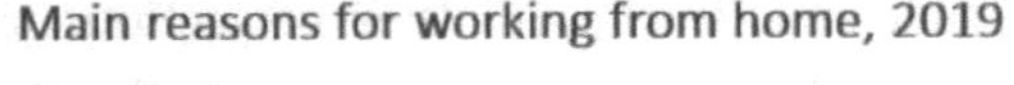

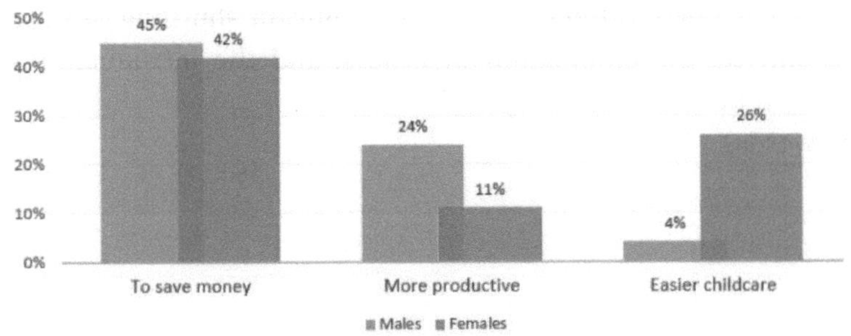

Hours worked from home, 2019		
Hours of work per week	**Males**	**Females**
Under 10	3%	74%
10 to 30	16%	22%
Over 30	81%	6%

Model answer

The bar chart illustrates the reasons men and women chose to work from home in 2019. Overall, saving money was the main reason for both males and females (45% and 42% respectively). In contrast, approximately a quarter of males put productivity as a reason, which was twice as high as the female response (24% and 11% respectively). For childcare, the pattern was different again with almost a quarter of females giving this reason compared to very few males (4%).

The table shows the hours men and women worked from home in 2019. The vast majority of males worked over 30 hours per week (81%) contrasting with a minority of females (6%) doing similar hours. This pattern is reversed when examining the under ten hours category with almost three quarters of females working this amount compared to only 3% of males. The 10 to 30 hours per week category shows fewer marked differences.

To sum up, it can be seen that men and women do not always give the same reasons for home working and, in general, men work longer hours from home.

(182 words)

9 798885 307482

Printed by Libri Plureos GmbH in Hamburg,
Germany